# We Need Mountains

# We Need Mountains

*Poems on Creation Care
and World Powers*

S T Kimbrough, Jr.

*Foreword by Will Willimon*

RESOURCE *Publications* · Eugene, Oregon

WE NEED MOUNTAINS
Poems on Creation Care and World Powers

Resource Publications
An Imprint of Wipf and Stock Publishers
199 W. 8th Ave., Suite 3
Eugene, OR 97401

www.wipfandstock.com

PAPERBACK ISBN: 978-1-6667-0084-8
HARDCOVER ISBN: 978-1-6667-0085-5
EBOOK ISBN: 978-1-6667-0086-2

05/17/21

# Contents

# Foreword

WHEN S T KIMBROUGH, Jr., looks at mountains, he sees more than the rest of us. Some poets teach the rest of us how to see, how to notice. Their poems open our eyes to the hidden wonder of things and give us the right words to say what we see and, by saying it well, enable us to see more than we would have seen unaided by their poetic vision. S T does that and more in this gracious, affirmative collection of his poems.

The poem that gives the title to this book exemplifies the remarkable way that S T's poetic vision enables him to see the human, moral significance in the world around him:

> For mountains can the spirit free
> from care and selfish pride.
> Their power, strength, and majesty
> should be a constant guide.

I've seen most of the mountains that have so inspired S T— Grand Tetons, Sand Mountain, the Blue Ridge—but I didn't see as much as he sees. S T really believes that even an inanimate thing like a mountain is imbued with the power to "free from care and selfish pride," even to the point of being our "guide." He looks at Mount Rushmore and sees both "grace and disgrace."

S T thinks that the natural world testifies to some of the worst of human inclinations. We drove the Iroquois, Shawnee, and Cherokee from these hills that today bring us inspiration. He lovingly gazes upon nature, all creatures great and small, and hears a call for human responsibility to the future of the world God has given us.

It's more than a little ironic that I write this, in the mountains (yes, along the rim of the Blue Ridge, looking toward the Smokies) isolated in a worldwide pandemic. I write this foreword as the same beneficent nature who grants us these beautiful mountains also hands us a pandemic, instigated by a virus, cousin of the common cold. If a mountain can speak, so a tiny pinpoint of a cell teaches us of our finitude and frailness, if we have the courage to learn its difficult lessons. From where I sit at the moment, these green mountains that look so blue in morning mist are doing better than we are. We who have done so much to undo nature's wonders for our own benefit may find ourselves undone by a virus.

In these poems S T beckons us to look with him, carefully to attend to the world, so that we may better care for the world in the future. He looks with a generous, grateful eye, finding wonders in creatures great and small. Traveling about the globe, S T sees us humans linked to the beauty of creation and to our despoliation of it. Not content to admire or wonder at the beauty of it all, S T moves from wonderment to assignment. God has graciously given us a hand in the care of God's world.

These poems will make you see and care about the world in fresh ways. Quite a gift.

**Will Willimon**
Professor of Christian Ministry
Duke Divinity School
United Methodist Church bishop, retired

# Introduction

ABOUT THREE-FOURTHS OF THE poems in this book concern themselves with the world around us which we need to protect and preserve. They are the necessary prelude to the importance of creation care, which I address specifically in the concluding poems. I am deeply grateful to my friend, Professor J. R. Watson, whose sensitive read-through of and response to these poems greatly enhanced the clarity of my intentions in addressing the timely subject of creation care.

A trip to Montana and Wyoming, particularly to Yellowstone National Park, accentuated again for me the absolute, breathtaking wonder of nature. To see regally poised buffalo spread across a wide terrain of mountains and meadows is a sight many a painter has captured, especially in western art of centuries past. To see the animals and natural beauty, however, far surpasses any artist's impression of nature's marvels.

There is something splendid, yet threatening, about pools of bubbling, boiling water, and vivacious geysers that seem to effervesce steam at both regular and irregular times. These are not human-created wonders; they are the wonders of creation.

The tall mountains and low valleys reveal temperatures of vast difference: on the highest mountaintops snowcaps freeze, and below, in the sun-blazed valleys of summer, vegetation flourishes, and in some places wheat and corn are harvested. In the snow-covered mountains of winter, the brown and black bears hibernate and Canadian geese fly south until springtime.

The season cycles in the mountains are a delight with the changing of tree-leaf colors. Riverbeds become almost dry from lack of rain, but in late spring they flow with the waters of melting snow. With each change of season, the sun circles the earth and sheds its light on places passed over in a previous season. This is experienced particularly in the mountain ranges of North America. They provide an amazing diversity of landscape, flora, and fauna. The various hues of the Blue Ridge Mountains and the Smoky Mountains are a delight to the eyes. The North American mountain ranges are also filled with stories of former Native American tribes, early settlers, wars, and "mountain men" of today.

Nature's creatures seem almost endless. Those of the springs and rivers and those of the forests fascinate us. In the fall salmon return to their rivers of origin and spawn new life. Diverse animal species fill the forests, meadows, and mountains with their newborn at various times of the year. In another book of poetry, *A Seagull Lunch and Other Nature Poems,* I have addressed many of the wonders of flora and fauna, which are captured here as well in "A Buffalo's Stare," "A Red-tailed Hawk," "Imagine Clouds," and others.

Part of the beauty of nature lies in its ever-changing, multiple scenes: "A Waterfall," "An Empty Beach," "Falling Leaves," "Magic Leaves," and "Fog, Go Away."

Perhaps we do not think of the "heavens" as harboring potential wonders of nature, but they are filled with the beauty of sunlight and moonlight, of sunrise and sunset, and the imaginary realm of clouds where we often imagine we see all sorts of images. The heavens are indeed "The World of Dreams." They may remind us also of what the weather portends: strong winds, rain, sleet, hail, and storms in many forms, hurricanes, cyclones, typhoons.

In these poems I have simply responded to nature's wonders around me.

> There's nothing that I would exchange
> for beauty all around:
> the iridescent skyward range
> of sunshine's broad rebound.
>
> . . .
>
> From nature, there's surprise that lasts
> day in, yes, and day out.

A charming spell on us it casts;
in this, it is devout.

Nature's art and music are all around us, if we but pause to see and hear.

The mix of sound includes an owl,
a nightingale's delightful song,
a single wolf's enchanting howl,
as nighttime concerts move along.

From time to time were learn of certain endangered species and of the conservationist's cry to protect the remaining few, that life may be protected, revived, and replenished. Often such efforts are effective. However, today there is a much broader and earnest cry for "Creation Care."

Creation care we must learn.
Creation for it groans.
Creation care, should we spurn,
perhaps we're left just stones.

Whether one travels north, south, east, or west, the evidence of global warming is prevalent.

"The glaciers crumble day by day,
the sea lions have no place to sun,
the newborn polar bears don't play
on ice sheets where they once had fun."
. . .
This breakdown nature now endures
results from dreadful human greed:
resisting fossil fuel cures,
the ozone layer's every need.

Will nature eventually lose one season or another because of human carelessness?

A world without a fall or spring,
and winter lost as well,
has only left the summer's sting
and temperatures of hell.

Unless the world powers step up and commit to preserving nature, the forthcoming catastrophes can be clearly seen through careful scientific analysis. The responsibility is in the hands of the world's most powerful nations.

> While China, India, USA
> let toxic gases have their way,
> the world looks on, indeed aghast,
> that these world powers let this last.

**S T Kimbrough, Jr.**

# Section One
# Nature's Mountains

## We Need Mountains

The alpine glow trims mountains red,
    beige, yellow, gold, and green.
These colors by sun-clouds are spread
    until the moon is seen.
At night, the moon shines on the snow,
    high on a mountain peak,
and paints as if it were van Gogh
    with color-born mystique.

At daybreak colors change again,
    and mountain life awakes.
Tree shadows slowly tend to wane,
    blue-green are now the lakes.
To breathe so deeply mountain air
    fresh from the lakes and trees,
and see a newborn elk or bear,
    one's spirit quickly frees.

For mountains can the spirit free
    from care and selfish pride.
Their power, strength, and majesty
    should be a constant guide.
The mountains no one may forget
    are central to life's course.
For water, food, we're in their debt.
    Take care of this life source!

## The Smoky Mountains

The mist of morning looks like smoke
    as it hangs in the air,
and I remember grandma spoke
    of how she'd sit and stare.
When only ten years old she'd sit
    on their front porch and look
at what she thought was smoke for sure
    with every glance she took.

They lived high on a mountain ridge,
    the valley down below,
She loved to cross a hanging bridge
    with her friend Mary Jo.
This way they reached the other side
    and walked right through the mist,
which grandma learned had not been smoke.
    How could she that have missed?

The Smoky Mountains was the name,
    she'd heard these mountains called,
and even school books made that claim,
    as often she recalled.
And yet there was no smoke to see,
    just nature's wistful touch
of snow-white vapor 'round each tree
    that grandma loved so much.

## Blue Ridge Mountains

From PA down to Georgia's line
    the Blue Ridge Mountains run.
They're filled with numerous mountain peaks,
    and parks for summer fun.
At Blowing Rock a tinge of blue
    reigns o'er the vast terrain.
As far as you can see this hue
    lays claim to its domain.

Here Iroquois and Shawnee tribes
    fished, hunted for their food,
but colonists and government bribes
    would force them out for good.
They must have loved the spruce-fir trees,
    the flora, fauna there,
but forced they were, brought to their knees,
    a treaty most unfair.

The Blue Ridge Mountains have a charm
    that never will be lost,
as long as humans do no harm
    at global warming's cost.
That black bears, songbirds, whitetail deer
    still roam this mountain range,
that wild boar, red fox, grouse still peer
    from forests is not strange.

The Shenandoah River calls
    as it rolls through the hills
and meets the wide Missouri falls
    and raging waters stills.
O Blue Ridge Mountains, cast your spell
    on all who trace your trails.
Let songs about your beauty swell
    and Blue-Ridge Mountain tales.

## A Rocky Mountain Story

The Rockies are the mountain range
    where I lived as a boy.
As immigrants, it was not strange
    the mountains to enjoy.
My mother came from Vietnam,
    my dad from a plateau
where he escaped the fierce napalm
    that devastated so.

The US brought as refugees,
    our family to the States.
This chance for us came not with ease;
    we wondered: What awaits?
High up the Rocky Mountain slopes,
    not far from Hopi tribes,
they settled us with brand-new hopes
    right where Rocky divides.

How fortunate an Asian child,
    learned English, Hopi too,
for when I spoke, my friends all smiled:
    "Teach us to speak like you!"
Vietnamese they also learned,
    this or that basic word,
and when we played, they often turned:
    "Is this the word I heard?"

My parents farmed the slopes each year;
      our crops were rich, we thrived.
Though sometimes winters were severe,
      like Hopis we survived.
They taught us things we did not know
      of the Great Spirit Guide:
this Spirit in the heaviest snow
      would give one strength inside:

To treasure Mother Earth each day,
      share with your friends your gain.
And even to a stranger say,
      "Welcome, we'll share our grain."
These things the Rockies, Hopis teach,
      life lessons far beyond
the words that we form in our speech:
      mountains simply respond.

## Lookout Mountain, Tennessee

On Lookout Mountain, Tennessee,
    I once stood as a boy,
where in year eighteen sixty-three
    the North/South troops deploy.
'Twas on November twenty-four
    the forces there engage;
and this would open wide the door
    a new campaign to stage.

Next day on Missionary Ridge
    the Union forces won
but struggled with a pontoon bridge
    and rebels on the run.
I knew not as a boy of this;
    the land now looked serene.
And one could all this history miss
    unless one sets the scene.

There are so many stories told
    how not so many died.
How soldiers, both the young and old,
    on both sides did collide.
And yet by night a moon eclipse
    let rebel forces flee.
In silence, all held tight their lips;
    good fortune, I agree.

I only know, as I stood there,
    I could not know the hate
that once the Civil War affair,
    would foster and dictate.
I stood there in my innocence,
    not having learned to hate.
God, save us from ambivalence,
    lest tolerance come too late.

## Sand Mountain

In Alabama there's a place,
    "Sand Mountain" called by name,
where folks a style of life embrace
    that many would disclaim.
There poverty spreads wide its net
    and health care's at a loss.
And wealthy folk dare not forget
    Sand Mountain bears a cross.

When I was young, Sand Mountain's fame
    had spread both far and wide,
a Christian sect had made the claim
    snakes are a spiritual guide.
"Snake Handlers" some did call them then,
    I do remember well.
The test of faith came to one when
    a snake bite made flesh swell.

If poisonous, it mattered not,
    one must be healed by prayer.
And should one die, all was for naught:
    one's faithlessness laid bare.
Authorities of state outlawed
    this practice inhumane;
revealed it as religion flawed,
    both secret and arcane.

It's sad Sand Mountain was made known
    by such a dangerous sect,
for many good folk there had sown
    life values quite correct.
The Methodists worked hard the land,
    and helped their neighbors out,
for justice learned to take a stand,
    and lived by faith, not doubt.

Sand Mountaineers, I do not mourn
    your past or unborn hope.
I simply pray: with words of scorn
    you must no longer cope.
The goodness in your souls I see,
    your faithfulness, hard work.
As Browning says with clarity:
    "Amend what flaws may lurk."

## The Grand Tetons

When standing still at Jackson Hole
    and looking toward the sky
I saw Wyoming's heart and soul,
    three peaks that fill the eye.
Though Grand Tetons they now are called,
    their first name Teewinot,
Shoshones gave them, it's recalled,
    three centuries ago.

The River Snake is down below,
    where waters swiftly run,
and there a young Shoshone boy
    fished, hunted in the sun.
The young boy's name Cameahwait,
    destined to be a chief,
canoeing learned, early and late
    and Shoshone belief.

Years later he met Lewis, Clark
    two men extraordinaire,
who, as explorers made their mark,
    and he became aware
of something he could scarce believe:
    his sister was their guide.
For her, he could for years but grieve;
    he thought for sure she'd died.

Sacagawea was her name,
          made hostage years before,
and now her brother she'd reclaim,
          lost years she'd now ignore.
Cameahwait fresh horses gave
          to Lewis and to Clark,
with thanks his sister, now no slave,
          on new life could embark.

Nostalgic is indeed the scene
          of Grand Tetons years past.
Cathedral-like, the sun-graced sheen
          on mountain peaks is cast.
Where can I native tribes now seek?
          Chief Cameahwait's long dead,
Montana's battle: Bloody Creek
          is where his last he bled.

As pastoral as the scene may be,
          and I observe it so,
we need to learn the history
          or we will never know
the truth and beauty of the folk
          who our forebears precede.
And we may cover, we may cloak
          the truth, ourselves mislead.

## Mountain Life

A mountain life is never dull,
 the plants and trees know tales
of life that's lived and always full
 along the mountain trails.
The loggers, hunters, trekkers too
 are lurking here and there
to make some cash or find a clue
 where one can trap a bear.

Then once there came some railroad men
 to blast a tunnel through,
the mountain trembled once, again,
 the birds, away they flew.
The hibernating bears awoke
 before the time had come,
and nature knew it was no joke:
 black bears would have no home.

One day a big, young trapper came
 to find a meadow wide,
to build a cabin, stake a claim
 for him and his new bride.
With timber cut, he'd cleared the land
 to build a house for two.
For mountain life they took a stand;
 it was for them, they knew.

Through every season, every change,
    the trapper and his wife
loved every tree and hillside range,
    which each year bring forth life.
While whippoorwills and nightingales
    sing on the mountain height,
the trapper and his wife tell takes
    each morning, noon, and night.

## An Appalachian Sage

The Appalachian Mountains run
    from north to south for miles.
Mount Mitchell rises toward the sun;
    but here there're many trials:
a dying industry of coal,
    a rampant lung disease,
and poverty that plagues the soul,
    and life is ill at ease.

There was a girl named Sally Jane
    born on our mountain side,
whose mother birthed her in the rain
    without a nurse or guide.
She was for sure the smartest girl
    that ever I did meet.
Her mother's name was Sarah Pearl,
    a disposition sweet.

The miracle of Sally Jane
    was all the words she knew;
hers was a dictionary brain,
    almost no word seemed new.
The alphabet she learned by heart
    when she was only three.
At four our teacher let her start
    to school by the oak tree.

One day a Bible salesman came
    to sell the Holy Word.
It was indeed an awful shame
    the Bible was unheard.
We had no preacher, had no church,
    but we had Sally Jane.
If she the Bible once could search,
    perhaps she'd make it plain.

The Bible salesman generously
    gave Sally Jane the book.
And daily very strenuously
    at page on page she'd look.
At words, new words, she'd never seen;
    she'd read aloud each page.
Oh yes, our Sally Jane was keen,
    an Appalachian sage.

Soon college opened wide its doors
    to our own Sally Jane.
We learned she made the highest scores,
    our Appalachian brain.
She studied medicine for years,
    but when those years were through,
to us returned, no doubts or fears;
    it was for her to do.

She's cared for us some twenty years;
    sometimes corn is her pay.
She sees us all as her own peers,
    and she's content to stay.
At evening-time you'll often hear
    her reading to a child,
pronouncing every word so clear,
    by words her life was styled.

Our Sally Jane personifies
        the stories that she's read.
This Good Samaritan relies
        on staying far ahead
of human need: "care for the sick
        the widow, and infirm"
she'd read and knew it was no trick,
        our sage would this confirm.

# The Adirondack Mountains

Atop a mountain named Whiteface
    in Adirondack's range
on clear days one sees space on space,
    and what at first seems strange,
for so high up your eyes can see
    Vermont and Montreal,
and slopes where families love to ski,
    the steeple of St. Paul.

The forests rich with giant trees,
    with deer and large, black bears
and honeycomb-producing bees,
    these Mother Nature shares.
Here native tribes lived long and well—
    Mohawk, Shoshone too,
Algonquin here at times did dwell,
    and traveled by canoe.

The hardened winters they endured
    are not to be compared
with wars the whites fought and procured
    terrain—no one was spared.
Then giant trees were often felled
    new settlements to build.
For natives who survived this spelled
    more grief the conquerors willed.

As if injustice were reversed,
　　casinos tribes now own,
and gambling rich folk have a thirst
　　such gambling to condone.
No gambling profits compensate
　　for lives and homeland lost.
and we are left to contemplate
　　the drastic human cost.

Since Adirondack mountains still
　　give nature yet a chance
with flora, fauna us to thrill,
　　we join in their romance.
The mountain romance bids each day
　　us love the forests green,
and cherish animals at play,
　　or gaze down a ravine.

## On Top of Old Smoky*

On top of old Smoky all covered with snow
I lost my true lover for courting too slow.
For courting's a pleasure and parting's a grief,
and a false-hearted lover is worse than a thief.
For a thief will just rob you and take all you save
But a false-hearted lover will lead you to the grave.
And the grave will decay you and turn you to dust.
Not one girl in a hundred a poor boy can trust.
They'll hug you and kiss you and tell you more lies
than cross-ties on a railroad or stars in the skies.
So, come, all you maidens, and listen to me,
never place your affections on a green willow tree.

Old Smoky's a riddle, Old Smoky's a tale,
that keeps you a-wond'rin' why she sent no mail.
You loved her and kissed her with love that was true.
You promised to love her, you thought she loved you.
The snow of the winter has now come and gone,
and when the snow melted, she left with the dawn.
Old Smoky, now tell me, where did I go wrong?
I know that I loved her with love that was strong.
A lover must tell you that she loves you too;
you'll love one another with love through and through.
I'll wait for the winter with snow all around
and here on Old Smoky true love may be found.

* Stanza 1, traditional; stanza 2 by S T Kimbrough, Jr.

## The Sierra Madre Mountains

The mountains, Sierra Madre,
    run California south to north.
One thinks not of them as tawdry,
    when one travels them back and forth.
The beauty one will discover:
    vast chaparral and oak woodlands,
evergreen forests that cover
    a habitat without demands.

It's here California's condor
    resides undisturbed from all view.
Of lands scarce developed, ponder:
    Will nature receive her just due?
Oil wells now in the south exist.
    the condors as yet have no threat.
But should oil firms further persist,
    they could the condors' lives upset.

The Sierra Madre Mountains,
    a nature's rarity, they are,
as rare as artesian fountains.
    Just look, they write their own memoir.
Sierra Mountain settlements
    are almost nowhere to be found.
But, oh, her mountain relishments
    in nature everywhere abound.

## Mount Rushmore

Democracy's Mount Rushmore shrine:
four presidents* shape the design.
Their faces on a mountain stand
Lakota Sioux thought holy land.
Some thought the face of Chief Red Cloud
would make the tribe Lakota proud.
Lewis and Clark or Buffalo Bill
others had claimed would add a thrill.
The Black Hills for Lakota Sioux
were sacred, but the gold breakthrough
would take away the sacred awe.
Lakotas lost to white man's flaw.
The sculptor Borglum's gifted art
showed talent from the very start.
The presidents he carved in stone
were gifted leaders on their own.
Each one democracy held high,
and for it Lincoln was to die.
The irony is with us still
as we gaze on the sculptor's skill.
The beauty of each stone-hewn face
is grace but also a disgrace,
for on Lakota sacred ground
four foreigners are sacred crowned.
Crowned as democracy's great shrine,
oft seen as freedom's great bloodline.

* George Washington (1732–1799), Abaham Lincoln
(1809–1865), Theodore Roosevelt (1858–1919), Thomas
Jefferson (1743–1826).

# The Wonder of Mountains

The mountains rise above the earth
    and regal stature bear.
Earth's molten lava gave them birth,
    forced peaks high in the air.

The mountains, valleys, peaks, and cliffs
    through ages came to be,
with chasms, gorges, giant rifts:
    amazing sights to see.

Some mountains sacred sights became,
    where people offered prayer.
And other mountains gained their fame
    from qualities found there.

The Smoky Mountains have no smoke,
    but mist of early dawn
looks like a smokescreen that might choke
    a doe and her young fawn.

The Blue Ridge Mountains are not blue,
    and yet at Blowing Rock
as far as you can see a hue
    of blue's enough to shock.

The mountains so enchanting are,
    they cast on us a spell
of beauty, wonder, near and far!
    Who can their splendor tell?

Section Two

# Nature's Creatures

## A Blue Jay Wins the Day

I walked about a mile today,
    and as I walked, I heard birds sing;
I saw two squirrels hard at play,
    and watched a cardinal take wing.

Before I sat down on my deck
    I filled my feeders with bird food.
The sparrows started seeds to peck.
    They seemed in such a pleasant mood.

Just then a big blue jay flew by
    to signal that he had arrived,
as if to say, "Sparrows, goodbye,"
    and swiftly toward the feeder dived.

The sparrows scattered in a flash
    escaping the blue jay's fierce beak.
The blue jay's action was quite brash,
    but preened a moment and looked chic.

A squirrel sat watching from a tree
    but did not dare attack the bird.
In this sparrows and squirrels agree:
    Attack a blue jay? That's unheard.

## A Buffalo's Stare

A buffalo stared face to face
        at me while I stood by.
Did he think, "You are in my space"?
        He looked by no means shy.

With strong black eyes and dark brown beard,
        and horns in regal stance,
he formed an image to be feared.
        I knew this at first glance.

His stare was long, intense, direct,
        his regal bearing strong.
Two small black birds his head bedecked
        and formed his royal throng.

He turned and sauntered on his way
        not looking back at me.
Yes, best it was he did not stay.
        Of his fierce stare, I'm free.

## A Flying Squirrel

A flying squirrel I'm sure I saw
    along a mountain trail.
A lizard hanging from its jaw
    was wagging fast its tail.

Of flying squirrels, I'd often heard
    but never one I'd seen.
I'd thought it surely was absurd,
    but saw him forward lean.

He perched a moment on a branch
    still holding tight his prey,
lunged forward like an avalanche
    and swiftly flew away.

## A Pelican, a Small Sand Crab

A pelican, a small sand crab
    meet on a sandy beach.
The big bird thinks the crab he'll grab,
    but it is out of reach.

It was a funny sight to see:
    the big bird in defeat.
The tiny crab began to flee,
    escape almost complete.

The pelican flapped after it;
    the crab bored in the sand.
The bird looked round: O little wit,
    it wasn't what he'd planned.

## A Red-tailed Hawk

A red-tailed hawk sat on my fence,
and lingered long, not flying hence.
At first, I thought he stared at me,
but wondered then: What does he see?
A large bay window stood between.
Had he his own reflection seen?
He flapped his wings as if quite proud.
To my surprise his screech was loud.
It seemed he paused for one more view,
then poised his wings and off he flew.

## A Seagull's Life

At dusk the seagulls dot the sand
    across the long, wide beach.
This way their rest nature has planned,
    a place to sleep for each.

They are not perched to fly away,
    their feet and wings tucked in.
They'll quiet stay till light of day,
    a new day to begin.

A day to soar into the air,
    to search along the sand,
to find a starfish, crab, here, there,
    and on one leg to stand,

To dive into the sea for fish,
    to find food to survive,
and if a seagull made a wish:
    'twould be, to stay alive!

## A Tiny Fawn

I saw a fawn across the street;
  it seemed to be alone.
It skipped and jumped on tiny feet,
  as it looked for its own.

The mother nowhere could be seen;
  the fawn was sick with fear;
its tiny body looked quite lean;
  unlike a full-grown deer.

It pushed against the garden gate
  but could not make it move.
It spun around, alas, too late,
  a break-in could not prove.

Across the road it quickly leapt,
  like lightning sped away.
At speed this fawn was quite adept,
  What more is there to say?

## What Magpies Do

A magpie gaily crossed the street
and hoped he'd find some food to eat.
But what the magpie did not know:
behind a pine tree stood a crow.
One crow-squawk and the magpie flew;
when threatened that's what magpies do.
They let a crow have its own way
and cross the street another day.

## Another Magpie

A Magpie's on my porch again
    to see what he can find.
It seems he won't much effort strain,
    appears to fate consigned.

I think his belly's rather full
    and hence his lazy search.
A brief peck at a piece of wool
    just left him in the lurch.

He nonchalantly pranced away
    as if he did not care.
But he'll be hungry the next day,
    so small birds should beware.

## Roast Goose?

Canadian geese delight in flight
    but when you're driving down the street,
and one struts into your headlight,
    you stop to miss those slow webbed feet.

The goose just takes his own good time,
    but fortune smiles, no car's behind.
You miss the goose, there's no goose crime,
    but just a moment bear in mind:

to swerve to miss a goose seems right,
    but if you cause an accident,
remember geese have no green light;
    you're guilty of the incident.

If safe, just let the goose pass by.
    If not, the choice is yours to make.
Roast goose is better than ask why
    you made this time a huge mistake.

## Ethereal Joy

The swallows and the swans at rest
    beside a quiet lake,
a willow tree harbors a nest
    that blue birds freshly make.

This placid scene at dusk I saw
    as moonbeams shadows cast
through trees like strands of wiry straw
    with light streaks traveling past.

Just then I heard a nightingale's
    melodious, rich song;
it was as if past fairytales
    made right the world of wrong.

I felt the magic nature wand
    transform my every thought:
it was, yes, an ethereal bond,
    a joy I had not sought.

## No Lunch

A red-winged blackbird met a crow
    beside a big wheat field.
But what the two birds did not know
    behind the wheat concealed
a large black cat lay on the ground
    quite ready for a meal.
It made no movement, not a sound,
    ready its lunch to steal.

Just then a field mouse scampered by;
    the two birds lunged at him.
The swift field mouse was much too sly;
    the bird attacks were grim.
As they collided in the air,
    the cat joined in the fray.
Thus, cat and birds the field mouse spare,
    and birds just fly away.

## A Rabbit and a Fox

A rabbit ran across my lawn
as sunlight signaled it was dawn.
I wondered why he spryly ran,
until as fast as Peter Pan
I saw a fox swift in the chase.
The rabbit, could it win the race?
The finish line I could not see;
my view was blocked by an oak tree.
I hope the rabbit got away
and lived to run another day.

# Section Three
# Nature's Scenes

## A Magic Spell

There's nothing that I would exchange
    for beauty all around:
the iridescent skyward range,
    the shadows on the ground,

When through the leaves of tall palm trees,
    I see a gulf wave break,
a sailboat leans as its crew frees
    it from a giant wake.

To see a child at its first touch
    of sand and sea-wave foam
is worth far more than gold or such
    if found where'er I roam.

A hang-glider on sea-skis soars,
    beneath a large balloon,
a symbol of life out of doors,
    to fear of heights immune.

From nature, there's surprise that lasts
    day in, yes, and day out.
A charming spell on us it casts;
    in this, it is devout.

## A Nature Concert of Rain

The rain fell on my roof with sounds
    of music with a beat.
The rhythms seemed to have no bounds.
    My, my! It was a treat.

As I lay there, this rain concert,
    a ticketless delight,
let nothing of my thoughts divert,
    especially by moonlight.

The moon peeked through the clouds of rain,
    as if softly to say,
"A nature's concert's not in vain,
    so listen night and day!"

## A Short Walk

Went for a walk today at three,
the wind blew fiercer by degree.
I quickly turned this way and that,
and then the wind blew off my hat.
I chased it down a cobbled street;
at last I trapped it with my feet.
I pulled it on till it felt tight,
not wanting with the wind to fight.
It's no surprise my walk was short
the fierce wind left me no resort.

## A Waterfall

A stream begins in a small spring
      that bubbles with intent:
to birth its winding, swift offspring,
      a river's first event.

It then is joined steam upon stream,
      and down the mountainside
each flows to make a silver dream
      of water, deep and wide.

Just then they came upon a cliff,
      with nowhere else to go,
There was no chance to ask, "What if?"
      They cascaded below.

Nearby a little boy cried out,
      "Mom, watch the water fall!"
That's how the name (How could one doubt?),
      was born, a waterfall.

## A Willow Tree

Beside a brook there stands a tree
    with weeping willow branches long.
They bend as if to make a plea
    to touch the brook that moves along,
As strong winds bend the branches down,
    some branches touch the water's edge;
as if the willow's life to crown
    the winds then whistle through the sedge.

To touch the water, what a treat,
    when slender, willow leaves are parched.
The water's touch relieves the heat,
    as branches gracefully are arched.
O willow, standing by the brook,
    your elegance is unsurpassed.
When I behold you, just one look,
    my spirit comes to life at last.

## An Empty Beach

An empty beach, without a soul,
    not ev'n a seagull seen,
no tiny crab digging a hole,
    not even sea grass green.
Than this, what can more lonely be?
    Just water, sand in sight!
Lone emptiness is all I see,
    but do I see aright?

Do I see what I want to see
    that mirrors my own soul?
If I have emptiness within,
    it will exact a toll
that hinders my own vision clear
    to see things as they are,
and I am left with vision drear,
    that bids sight *au revoir*.

But look again at the lone beach;
    there's beauty all around.
The clouds seem like they want to reach
    the shore and touch the ground.
The moon is waning as the sun
    shines like a radiant gem.
The waves are slowly on the run,
    a jeweled diadem.

## Dish Divine

The leaves are green, the sap will rise,
    and soon we'll tap the trees.
In a few days, we'll gain the prize:
    More maple syrup, please.

The syrup is delectable;
    I'll savor every taste.
No bitterness detectable;
    no, not a drop I'll waste.

I'll take the pail, stick in my thumb
    and taste this dish divine.
And, oh, how blissful the outcome,
    on such a dish to dine.

## Falling Leaves

The leaves now left on post oak trees
    beyond my window pane,
no doubt will not survive the freeze,
    or hail, or winter rain.

In fall they turned both yellow, red
    and gave me such a thrill.
But now they're brown and seem quite dead
    caused by the winter's will.

Yet even so, the brown ones fall,
    oft guided by their shape.
Some speedily descend, if small;
    if large, float like a cape.

To watch each leaf float and descend,
    a gift of nature's art,
most surely can a sad mood mend,
    breathe joy into the heart.

## Magic Leaves

The reddened, glistening maple leaves
fly here and there under the eaves.
As autumn wind moves them around,
bright colors here and there abound.
Some yellow oak leaves join the mix,
as brown, magenta ones play tricks.
They fly so gently through the air,
like floating angels unaware.
They're unaware of wind and rain,
and happy that it's fall again.
The winter welcomes barren trees,
and here and there a shivering freeze.
When springtime comes the trees will bud,
as nature sends them new-life blood.

## An Autumn Blanket of Color

The trees beyond my porch turn red
    and yellow, orange and brown,
as nature's autumn blanket's spread
    and leaves come floating down.

The floating leaves, a bright array
    of colors in the air,
are topped by snowflake's white display,
    a sight beyond compare!

The leaves alight upon the grass,
    which quickly fills with snow,
and lovely whiteness comes to pass,
    and colors have to go.

## Fog, Go Away!

Fog spreads across the rippling bay;
    the ripples though I cannot see,
I hear them as I go my way,
    as once I heard on Saint Marie.

The fog comes in and then goes out,
    as if it wants to play a game
and tempt the sailors all to doubt,
    or make each one the weather blame.

The weather blame: "no sail today,"
    that's posted at their sailing shed,
"The fog's too thick," goes on to say,
    "it's time to clean your boats instead."

"O dreary fog, just go away,
    don't ruin another sailing race!
And, sun, please burn away the gray
    and put the thick fog in its place!"

## Forest Music

The sound of trees blown by the wind,
    the whirring of a stone-filled stream,
the forest as you stroll will send
    your way, as if it were a dream.

The mix of sound includes an owl,
    a nightingale's delightful song,
a single wolf's enchanting howl,
    as nighttime concerts move along.

In nature's own orchestral sounds
    there's pleasure; listen, you will hear
that forest music rich abounds:
    enchanting music fills the ear.

## A Garden of Dreams

There is a garden filled with dreams;
its colors make it more it seems,
    than one might dare to think.
The tall green ferns, the roses red,
the buttercups white, yellow wed
    with sweet peas dazzling pink.

Just one walk through, my troubled soul
had never dreamed to feel so whole.
    Then fragrances divine
created sense there is a chance
to lift my spirit, make it dance,
    and say, "This dance is mine."

## One Uneasy Morn

The gray clouds touch the tops of trees,
  the sun shines dimly through,
the fog creeps in itself to please
  and veils the morning dew.

The shoreline can one scarcely see,
  though breaking waves, one hears.
A foghorn sounds for those at sea,
  to guide in spite of fears,

Of fears that lurk beneath the waves
  for ships on nearby course;
the foghorn's sound both guides and saves
  ships' crews from deadly force.

Then suddenly the clouds recede;
  the fog soon disappears.
The foghorn's "all clear" ships then heed,
  as crews cast off their fears.

## The Stolen Winds

The winds against the tall, bare trees,
    whose leaves it's fiercely shorn,
bends down their limbs with facile ease,
    till finally breaks the morn.

The forceful winds gave no relief
    until the break of day,
then vanished as if by a thief
    were stolen, whisked away.

## Reflections

Upon a giant crater lake
      are mirrored such delightful scenes:
a redwood tree, make no mistake,
      though it appears upright, it leans.

Reflections one sees of a bear
      that roams along the rocky shore.
It stops a moment just to stare,
      snaps up a fish, then tries for more.

Majestic are the giant trees
      that seem to bend on rippling waves,
but rushing winds change all one sees;
      the wind reflections never saves.

But for some moments one may see
      reflections charming to the eyes,
and what was not, may come to be,
      until the gusts of wind revise.

## Off to Tanzania

To climb Mount Kilimanjaro
    requires much strength, preparation,
for most a dream for tomorrow
    with thoughts of self-adulation.

The travel to Tanzania
    in Africa's wild, distant East,
you soon will find may be a
    tough test of endurance at least.

If climbing's not your cup of tea,
    perhaps on a Safari ride
you'll have a unique chance to see
    some lions lying side by side.

If not, the wind against your face,
    fresh air you breathe beyond compare,
from Africa will leave a trace,
    if nothing more than windblown hair.

## All the Same

Silk-coated clouds on breaths of blue
float softly on gentle puffs of wind,
while geese fly south in annual tableau
of nature's artistic, stunning skill.
Year by year, canvas by canvas,
painters try to capture the scene,
always the same, yet always different.
We think we see nature's sameness,
but what seems the same is never so.
The annual migration of Wildebeests,
is it not the same time each year, the same route?
Little ones, the look-a-likes, have grown,
older ones died, others were a lion's meal.
Each year cranes return to the same lakes,
sea turtles bury their eggs on the same beach.
We are born, we grow, we live, we die,
just the same as everyone before us:
All the same, yet, never the same.

## Where Can the Soul Be Satisfied?

Where can the soul be satisfied—
    in nature by a flowing stream
where birds sing, flowers grow beside
    the rustling waters as they gleam?

The gleam from sunshine through the trees
    makes sparkles on the stream like gems.
To live in moments such as these
    one knows that joy from nature stems.

What solace on a mountain peak
    one finds in quietness serene.
One needs no single word to speak
    for breathtaking, the nature scene.

The beauty of the desert sand
    is sleek and endless, peaceful, bare.
Though sandstorms rise without command,
    the majesty of nature's there.

In nature we're endowed with grace
    and, if we will, o'erwhelmed with joy;
each bird-song, brook will us embrace,
    a link essential, said Tolstoy.

## A Weeping Birch Tree

A weeping birch tree stands beside
    our house on Stockton Street.
Its giant, arching branches glide
    from blue sky to your feet.

The arching branches shield a space
    from sun and from the rain;
and children rush to claim this place
    as their own play domain.

To stand within this charming spot,
    that nature's skill creates,
helps humans see their happy lot
    as nature's advocates.

## Bluebonnets

Bluebonnets fill the meadowland
and make of it a wonderland.
They fill the valley with rich blue;
oh, what delight as I walk through.
My spirit floats as on a cloud,
such beauty gloriously endowed!
As far as I can see there's blue;
oh, what an other-worldly view.
I wish that I could stop all time
and bask in moments so sublime.

# Wonder

The intonation of small steps
    makes music in the night;
the ocean still, moonlight accepts,
    as Jane steps into light.

The quiet touch of ocean waves
    plays wistfully on shore,
as moonlight gently so behaves,
    that Jane would long for more.

Yes, more of the enchanting light
    reflecting from the sea,
that not a ripple seems to slight,
    as sea and moon agree.

The dance of moon and light sea spray,
    a marvel for young Jane,
makes beauty sing, and lets her play
    and dance, and skip again.

Through wonder what life means is plain.
    No wonder? What's life worth?
No wonder? "Oh my, no!" says Jane.
    "No wonder, there's no mirth!"

No wonder, then no happiness;
    no smiles upon the face.
No wonder, life is meaningless;
    in wonder is life's grace.

## A Water Lily

A water lily is sheer bliss,
caressed by water's tender kiss.
It gently floats upon a pond,
as if made by a magic wand.
Its beauty can enchant the soul;
its beauty can a heart console.
Its petals' white, magenta hues
oft sparkle through the morning dews.
The lilies float but scarcely move;
their roots of movement disapprove,
except for ripples on the pond.
Of these slight movements they are fond.
O water lily, floating there,
I'm blessed your beauty I can share.

# Glowing Treetops

The glowing treetops in sunlight
     with snow sparkle and gleam.
A nearby lake mirrors delight
     from sunlight's daily scheme.

The sunlight's scheme is a design
     that sheds light everywhere,
except when shadows dark align
     the sunlight to impair.

But glowing treetops easily
     escape the shadow's snare,
for so high up repeatedly
     treetops catch sun's first flare.

## Serenity

The quiet rush of waves on shore,
    a gentle eastern breeze,
my spirit lift and o'er me pour
    both calm and unknown ease.

As quietly the realm of calm
    embraces me with peace,
I sense the touch of nature's balm,
    complete, complete release,

release from this world's frantic pace,
    its tensions, highs and lows,
for by the sea I find the space
    where calmness grows and grows.

Serenely now the realm of calm
    extends its warm embrace,
and all my life, without a qualm,
    serenity I'll trace.

## A Wordless Sunset

A wordless sunset awesome is;
 I too am without words,
and also is my good friend, Liz,
 but not the evening birds.

At dusk the cheerful nightingale
 resounds its haunting song,
the whippoorwill expands the scale
 as sunset moves along.

As nature's cycle turns and turns
 across the planet earth
the joy of nature's art one learns
 and every moment's worth.

Observe a sunset, hear the birds,
 the dazzling colors see,
as poets struggle with the words
 that beauty would set free.

Section Four

# Nature's Heavens

## Clouds

The clouds above in gray and white
    surround the mountain range;
while some seem still, others take flight,
    the pale-white ones look strange.

One giant plume of white unfolds
    as if it soon would burst.
A black cloud turns, surrounds, and holds
    the white cloud, as if cursed.

A burst of thunder, lightning flash,
    disburse the white cloud's charm,
and boisterous rain and hail's loud crash
    anticipate some harm.

When rain and hail have run their course,
    white clouds appear again.
It seems they're driven by a force
    that rain, hail will restrain.

A world of wonder they create
    of figures and of forms:
a giant nose, a big round plate,
    a dancer who performs.

Clouds are not always what they seem,
    hence, we imagine thus:
we see in them dream upon dream,
    enchanting all of us!

# Imagine Clouds

Imagination is a gift
    that clouds in us renew.
From them our spirits gain a lift
    from thoughts that are brand-new.

One sees in clouds the unforeseen,
    the magic of their forms.
Quite suddenly a forest green
    transforms to giant storms.

The unforeseen is a surprise,
    to see what you don't see,
but clouds can often in disguise
    reveal stark clarity.

Disguises show us the unseen,
    the sheep that was not there,
a lion with a scary mien,
    a brown bear in its lair.

Imagine this, imagine that,
    clouds constantly invite,
a jaguar, dog, a mouse, a cat,
    look up, oh, what a sight!

## Wandering Clouds

The sky is filled with tumbling clouds
    that seem to wander to and fro.
One group looks like it's gathering crowds
    of dark clouds with no place to go.
Strange, giant clouds constantly move
    and gather o'er tumultuous seas.
Does Mother Nature wish to prove
    she's in control of scenes like these?

If I could wander like a cloud
    and float and soar to heights unseen,
somehow, I think I would be proud,
    and dream I'd reached the in-between—
between the mortal realm and realm
    of nature, I'd most surely be,
but then discover at the helm
    there's nature's stark reality.

To wander like a cloud's a dream
    no human being can achieve,
but mortals' minds have gifts to stream
    imagination and believe
the world is more than what we see;
    it's more than all our words describe.
It's an enchanting mystery,
    that humans daily can imbibe.

## In Flight

From thirty thousand meters high
    I see the rivers down below.
Such beauty one cannot deny,
    their snakelike, winding constant flow.

Along their banks are houses, towns,
    all which were built by human hands.
It seems they all have ups and downs:
    one old house falls, another stands.

By human hands rivers weren't made,
    the oldest ones I know by name.
I see their waters brown, green, jade,
    and river routes, never the same.

How tiny this world seems to me,
    from thirty thousand meters high,
but landing, all at once I see,
    the world I just saw from the sky.

## Light Travel

This morning's rhapsody of light
    on oceans, bays, and streams
is nature's dance and soaring flight
    of rays and flickering beams.

The light refractions tease the eyes,
    if they would follow them.
One glance, and then a thousand tries
    or was it just a whim?

A dash of light like shooting stars
    soars on in swift light years.
I look, alas, it's gone to Mars,
    perhaps ev'n Pluto nears.

Would I could travel with this light
    beyond earth's atmosphere,
I'd wonder, wonder if I might
    light travel learn to steer!

## Sunset

At dusk the sunset charms the bay
　　as colors change, then die.
A fading orange turns to gray;
　　on change sunsets rely.

The fringe of red atop a cloud
　　reveals the waning sun;
a shadowed shoreline like a shroud
　　enfolds a day that's done.

A sunset is dependable;
　　it daily comes to pass.
Its art is not expendable;
　　it's for the world *en masse*.

Photographers and painters too
　　would capture sunset art;
yet better with one's eyes to view,
　　inspires and thrills the heart.

The colors dance upon the bay
　　before the sun descends,
and what a vast color buffet
　　each sunset often lends.

The darkness never quite descends
　　without the sunset's mark.
Yet darkness cannot make amends
　　ev'n with a singing lark.

## The World of Clouds

The clouds in giant plumes of white
    caress the snow-capped mountain peaks.
They kiss remaining snow in sight;
    their vapor veils the mountain creeks.

How must it be within a cloud
    to travel miles above the earth
with no one there to speak out loud,
    and there is neither pain nor mirth?

Like magic carpets of the East
    some clouds fly on at rapid speed:
they fly, the greatest and the least,
    as if the winds and gales to heed.

Some clouds, however, seem quite still,
    as though they have no place to go.
It seems that they have their own will;
    and hence form their own cloud tableau.

## Heavenly Art

The clouds above need speak no words,
     they easily communicate.
Some picture jugs brimming with curds
     or sheep in line before a gate.

The weather is the artist, whose
     own energy helps paint the sky.
The wind, clouds, sun, morn, dusk may choose
     the colors that will satisfy.

The colors, mainly white, grey, black,
     except when sunlight turns clouds gold;
no beauty, elegance they lack.
     This heavenly art is ages old.

Some clouds seem friendly, intimate,
     while others threaten us with storms.
I watch them gladly turn, rotate,
     and try to guess what each cloud forms.

I lie upon my back and stare
     at clouds that change their shape above.
What art would anyone compare
     with such a sign of heaven's love?

Section Five

# Nature's Care

## Creation Care

Health care is a common theme
    one hears of day by day.
Creation care it would seem
    some say we should delay.

One hopes people understand
    how crucial is this care.
The rivers, seas, also land
    will die unless we dare,

we dare challenge climate change,
    more gently treat the earth.
Recycle till it's not strange.
    Give clean air a new birth.

There's Styrofoam: cups and plates,
    grave hazards both are they.
Creation friends long awaits,
    who misuse will gainsay.

Green energy we should buy,
    no incandescent light.
Then we'll see the reason why
    this makes sense day and night.

Creation care we must learn,
    creation groans and groans.
Creation care should we spurn,
    perhaps we're left just stones.

## Mother Nature's Frown

A traveler journeys to the north
    the arctic beauty to behold.
He quickly learns as he goes forth
    what scientists for decades told:
"The glaciers crumble day by day,
    the sea lions have no place to sun,
the newborn polar bears don't play
    on ice sheets where they once had fun."

The traveler sees that this is true;
    the glaciers trimmed in ugly brown
each minute lose their natural hue,
    as beauty suffers a breakdown.
This breakdown nature long endures
    results from dreadful human greed:
resisting fossil fuel cures,
    the ozone layer's desperate need.

## Were It Not So!

Outside my window leaves turned gold
    now flutter, and then drop.
The autumn comes, and then the cold;
    the seasons never stop.

Unless we human carelessness
    with fossil fuels spurn,
then we will know the senseless mess
    from climate-change we'll learn.

The autumn may not come at all
    and winter vanish too.
No rain, no snow, no leaves that fall,
    a tragic, new worldview.

A world without a fall or spring,
    and winter lost as well,
has only left the summer's sting
    and temperatures of hell.

## Where's Winter?

It's January where I am,
    and temperatures are warm.
Is winter this year on the lam?
    We've seen not one snowstorm.

My garden's filled with flower buds.
    Their bulbs think spring has come,
and yet, there are no springtime floods.
    The weather's so humdrum.

The sun is shining, there's no snow.
    The weather's balmy here,
and soon the grass I'll have to mow,
    if winter won't appear.

## World Powers

When glaciers feed no water flow,
and global warming hinders snow,
the irony is oceans rise,
and island nations fear demise.
While China, India, USA
let toxic gases have their way,
the world looks on, indeed aghast,
that these world powers let this last.
Is nothing of a conscience left?
Is evidence of science bereft?
Wake up, world powers, in your hands
lies destiny of global lands.

## The River Nile

How could it be the River Nile,
 that south to north Africa spans,
in a few years, in a brief while,
 to clean pollution will need plans?

Need plans to make the water clean
 for drinking, bathing, or to cook.
Things cannot stay the way they've been;
 one sees this clearly with one look.

In Cairo many living there
 fear water from the Nile to drink,
and others may not be aware
 the Nile has more waste than you think.

Untreated chemicals are there,
 that come from agriculture's waste;
and population spikes won't spare
 more time; officials must make haste.

The Nile for centuries life's source
 has been for Egypt and Sudan,
for Ethiopia a force,
 Burundi whence its flow began.

All life on water does depend;
 this primal source can life sustain.
The nations must their rivers mend
 lest only riverbeds remain.

## Unknown

Sun, stars, and moon in deep, dark blue
    within a galaxy, how old?
Was there a time creation threw
    the galaxies a hundredfold
across space-time the way to clear,
    that lodestars, ev'n the Bethlehem star
to seamen, wise men might appear?
    Galaxies' unknown repertoire
of purposes, a mystery,
    intrigues the mind beyond compare,
stirs intellect with inquiry:
    Have we too there a role of care?

## Pollution

Pollution left, pollution right,
pollution scarcely out of sight.
Pollution's dire effects are real
on health, emotions, how we feel.
It wrecks the ecosystem's chance
for flora, fauna, to advance.
Pollution thrives on wealth and greed
and negligence of human need.
The streams and rivers filled with trash
diseases breed that with health clash.
When streams and rivers overflow
with garbage so fish, plants can't grow,
and landscape beauty long succumbs,
a forest barren soon becomes,
we reap pollution's dire result:
humanity's grave, worst insult.
Pollution can our lives deprive
of what we need to stay alive.

## Guests of Eternity

We're guests here of eternity,
　　but guest-stays here aren't free.
We have responsibility
　　for guests who're yet to be.

The forests, rivers, city streets,
　　the drinking water too,
"Their preservation," one repeats,
　　"depends, depends on you."

There's also hospitality
　　with open arms to all;
and practice of fidelity
　　to lift up those who fall.

To say for these things, we've no time,
　　insults eternity,
and makes our guest-stay here a crime
　　and us absurdity.

www.ingramcontent.com/pod-product-compliance
Lightning Source LLC
LaVergne TN
LVHW051701080426
835511LV00017B/2664